Making a Web Page

By Colleen van Lent and Christopher van Lent

CHERRY LAKE
Publishing

Published in the United States of America by
Cherry Lake Publishing
Ann Arbor, Michigan
www.cherrylakepublishing.com

Series Editor: Kristin Fontichiaro
Reading Adviser: Marla Conn, MD, Ed., Literacy Specialist,
Read-Ability, Inc.
Photo Credits: Cover, ©Gladskikh Tatiana/Shutterstock; all other
images by Colleen van Lent.

Library of Congress Cataloging-in-Publication Data
Names: Van Lent, Colleen, author.
Title: Making a web page / by Colleen van Lent and Christopher van Lent.
Description: Ann Arbor, Michigan : Cherry Lake Publishing, 2018. | Series: Makers as
   innovators junior | Includes bibliographical references and index.
Identifiers: LCCN 2017031215 | ISBN 9781534107809 (lib. bdg.) | ISBN 9781534109780
   (pdf) | ISBN 9781534108790 (pbk.) | ISBN 9781534120778 (ebook)
Subjects: LCSH: Web sites—Design—Juvenile literature.
Classification: LCC TK5105.888. V363 2018 | DDC 006.7—dc23
   LC record available at https://lccn.loc.gov/2017031215

Cherry Lake Publishing would like to acknowledge the work of the Partnership for
21st Century Learning. Please visit *www.p21.org* for more information.

Printed in the United States of America
Corporate Graphics

A Note to Adults: Please review the instructions for the activities in this book before allowing children to do them. Be sure to help them with any activities you do not think they can safely complete on their own.

A Note to Kids: Be sure to ask an adult for help with these activities when you need it. Always put your safety first!

Table of Contents

```
<!DOCTYPE html>
<html lang="en">
<head>
    <meta charset="UTF-8">
    <title>Making a Web Page</title>
</head>
<body>
    <h1>Christopher van Lent</h1>

    <p>I <i>like</i> pizza.</p>

    <p>I <b><i>love</i></b> to play
    video games.</p>

    <img src = "BaconTheDog.JPG" alt = "Bacon"

    style = "float: right; width:20%">

</body>
</html>
```

Take your first peek at HTML. Can you crack the code? Turn to page 16 to see what this code looks like as a web page!

What Is HTML?

People like to use the Internet to play and learn. Have you ever wondered how web pages are made? They are created using a programming language called **HTML**. HTML can tell a computer what to do. The computer uses these instructions to make things look a certain way on your screen.

Christopher van Lent I like pizza. I love to play video games.

This web page is boring and ugly. We can use HTML to make it better.

Writing Code

You can use a special program called an **editor** to write **code** for a web page. Another program called a **browser** lets you look at the web page. Let's type something in an editor:

```
Christopher van Lent

I like pizza.

I love to play video games.
```

This is just regular English! If you open it with a browser, it looks like the image to the left.

Christopher van Lent

I like pizza.

I love to play video games.

Only the text in between a set of tags will be changed by the tags.

All About Tags

Our code is missing **tags**. Tags are an important part of HTML. They tell the browser how your web page should look. Most tags have two parts. These are the opening tag and the closing tag. Let's try changing our code as shown to the left.

Christopher van Lent

I like pizza. I love to play video games.

Look! The <h1> tag makes our page look better already.

Heading Tags

It worked! The <h1> tag is called a heading tag. Have you figured out what it does? It shows that the first line you wrote is important. It makes these words big and bold. It also puts them on a separate line from everything else.

Only the first line is between the <h1> and </h1> tags. Notice that the other lines don't change.

Creating with Code

What exactly is code? Code is something you write for computers, not people. You can only see the tags in your editor. They will not show up when your web page is opened in a browser.

Christopher van Lent

I like pizza.

I love to play video games.

Can you see what the <p> does? We made two paragraphs!

Putting Paragraphs on the Page

Now we need to stop the browser from putting the last two lines together. We can do this with paragraph tags. Each <p> starts a new paragraph. A </p> tag ends the paragraph.

```
<h1>Christopher van Lent</h1>

<p>I like pizza.</p>

<p>I love to play video
games.</p>
```

Now the lines are separated! Check it out to the left.

Christopher van Lent

I *like* pizza.

I **love** to play video games.

Look closely. The words *like* and **love** look different now.

Bold and Italic Text

Christopher *likes* pizza. He ***loves*** to play video games. How can we show this? We can use <i> tags for italic and <b> tags for bold.

```
<h1>Christopher van Lent</h1>
<p>I <i>like</i> pizza.</p>
<p>I <b><i>love</i></b> to
play video games.</p>
```

Oops!

A closing tag needs a "/". People often forget to include it. This is a big mistake. A browser can't figure out where the tag ends without it. If something isn't working right on your web page, check to make sure you used closing tags.

Christopher van Lent

I *like* pizza.

I **love** to play video games.

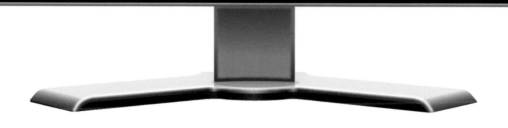

Remember the code you first saw on page 4? It was used to make this page! Images can be tricky, but our dog Bacon is too cute to leave off our web page.

Picture-Perfect

The <img> tag lets you put an image on your page. This tag needs extra information called an **attribute**. The "src" attribute tells the <img> tag which picture we want.

We have a lot of pictures of our dog, Bacon, on our computer. We want the one named "BaconTheDog.jpg".

```
<img src = "BaconTheDog.jpg">
```

A Different Kind of Tag

Do you notice a difference between <img> and the other tags we've used so far? Unlike the others, <img> does not need a closing tag. That's because it is something called a self-closing tag.

Christopher van Lent

I *like* pizza.

I **love** to play video games.

Which colors will you use on your page?

Coding with Style

You can also use attributes to change the way your page looks. The "src" attribute told the browser where to find an image. You can use the "style" attribute to change the size or color of something. Try this code:

```
<h1 style =
"color:blue">Christopher van
Lent</h1>

<p style = "color:green">I
<i>like</i> pizza.</p>

<p>I <b><i>love</i></b> to
play video games.</p>
```

Our friends love to share their images online. They leave out their last names so they stay safe online.

Keep Going!

If you like coding, you can make a web page! You only need a little bit of HTML and some imagination.

Will you make a web page about your school? Your pet? Your favorite stuffed animal? Your art projects? Or maybe a fun family vacation? Don't worry if you make mistakes. Just have fun!

Glossary

attribute (AT-rih-byoot) a part of a tag that gives a browser extra information

browser (BROW-zur) a program used to surf the web and display HTML files; common examples include Edge, Safari, Chrome, and Firefox

code (KODE) instructions for a computer, written in a special language

editor (ED-uh-tur) a program used to create HTML files; WordPad or TextEdit can be found on most computers

HTML (AITCH TEE EM EL) a computer language that is mainly used to create web pages; HTML is short for "hypertext markup language"

tags (TAGZ) pieces of HTML code that are used to organize things on a web page, change the page's appearance, or provide a browser with other important information

Find Out More

Books
Van Lent, Colleen. *Web Design with HTML5.* Ann Arbor, MI: Cherry Lake Publishing, 2015.
Van Lent, Colleen. *More Web Design with HTML5.* Ann Arbor, MI: Cherry Lake Publishing, 2015.

Web Sites
Envato Tuts+ Web Design for Kids: Getting Ready to Build a Website
https://webdesign.tutsplus.com/tutorials/web-design-for-kids-getting-ready-to-build-a-website–cms-23762
Check out some more advanced tips for planning and building a website.

Learning HTML for Kids
www.goodellgroup.com/tutorial/toc.html
Learn even more about editors, code, and ways to make your page even better with lists, links, and formatting.

Index

About the Authors

Colleen van Lent teaches programming at the University of Michigan.
Christopher van Lent is a middle school student who likes to code and play
video games. They have a dog named Bacon.